BULLDOGS

KATIE LAJINESS

BIG BUDDY DOGS

Big Buddy Books
An Imprint of Abdo Publishing
abdopublishing.com

abdopublishing.com

Published by Abdo Publishing, a division of ABDO, PO Box 398166, Minneapolis, Minnesota 55439.

Printed in China.
092017
012018

THIS BOOK CONTAINS RECYCLED MATERIALS

Cover Photo: Getty Images.
Interior Photos: AP Photo/ Martin Mejia (p. 29); Drew Angerer/Getty Images (p. 5); Getty Images (pp. 9, 11, 13, 15, 17, 19, 21, 23, 25, 27); Jen Boner (pp. 7, 30).

Coordinating Series Editor: Tamara L. Britton
Contributing Editor: Jill Roesler
Graphic Design: Jenny Christensen

Publisher's Cataloging-in-Publication Data

Names: Lajiness, Katie, author.
Title: Bulldogs / by Katie Lajiness.
Description: Minneapolis, Minnesota : Abdo Publishing, 2018. | Series: Big buddy dogs | Includes online resources and index.
Identifiers: LCCN 2017943932 | ISBN 9781532112065 (lib.bdg.) | ISBN 9781614799139 (ebook)
Subjects: LCSH: Bulldog--Juvenile literature. | Dogs--Juvenile literature.
Classification: DDC 636.72--dc23
LC record available at https://lccn.loc.gov/2017943932

CONTENTS

A POPULAR BREED

Dogs are popular pets. About 44 percent of households in the United States have a dog. And Americans own more than 78 million total!

Around the world, there are more than 400 dog **breeds**. One of these is the bulldog. Let's learn why the bulldog is the country's fourth-most popular breed.

In 2017, a bulldog won Best of Breed at the Westminster Kennel Club Dog Show.

THE DOG FAMILY

Dogs come in all shapes and sizes. Yet all dogs belong to the **Canidae** family. The name comes from the Latin word for dog, which is *canis*. This family includes coyotes, foxes, wolves, and more.

Humans and dogs have lived together for at least 16,000 years. In the beginning, humans **bred** them to hunt. Soon, they trained dogs to do other jobs such as guarding property and herding livestock.

The wrinkles on a bulldog's face help drain blood away from the face and mouth.

BULLDOGS

The bulldog's **ancestors** were large dogs called mastiffs. In the beginning bulldogs were known to fight bulls. Sometimes, they were even used in war.

In 1835, new laws put an end to bull fighting. After that, humans raised bulldogs to be kind animals. Over time, the **breed** began to appear in the United States. In 1886, the bulldog joined the **American Kennel Club (AKC)**.

The bulldog breed nearly vanished once bull fighting ended. However, a small group of breeders saved the bulldog.

Two of America's past presidents had pet bulldogs. Warren Harding named his bulldog Old Boy. And Calvin Coolidge named his dog Boston Beans.

Today, many schools use the bulldog as their **mascot**. Yale University has a bulldog mascot. So does The Citadel.

Did you know?

Today, there are both English and French bulldogs. However, the word *bulldog* by itself generally refers to the English bulldog.

The bulldog mascot at Yale University goes by the name Handsome Dan.

WHAT THEY'RE LIKE

Bulldogs are kind, gentle dogs. They are also loyal family companions. But, bulldogs can have problems, too. They can be moody and difficult to train. Sometimes, they do not want to obey their owners or learn new tricks.

Bulldogs are sensitive dogs. They do not like teasing, pinching, or playing rough.

COAT AND COLOR

A bulldog's coat is short and smooth. An individual dog can be one of many colors. A bulldog's hair can be white, red, tan, or **fawn**. It can also be **brindle** or **piebald** patterned.

Did you know?

The AKC includes the bulldog in the Non-Sporting Group. Non-Sporting dogs include different breeds, sizes, and coats.

A bulldog's coat can be one of ten different combinations of colors and patterns.

SIZE

Bulldogs are heavyset dogs with strong legs. Their heads, chests, and hips are also big. Males weigh about 50 pounds (23 kg). Female bulldogs are smaller.

These are medium-sized dogs. A bulldog has small, floppy ears and a short, curly tail. The males stand about 12 to 15 inches (30 to 38 cm) tall at the shoulder. The females are somewhat smaller.

Bulldogs do not bark very often. Their noses are short, so they snort and wheeze. And, they snore loudly!

FEEDING

All dogs need food and water to supply energy. Quality dog food provides important **nutrients**. Dogs can eat moist, semimoist, and dry foods. Puppies eat three or more small meals a day. Adult dogs eat one to two times a day.

These dogs can be messy eaters. Feed a bulldog in the kitchen or outside for easy cleanup.

CARE

All dogs require good care. Many people recognize bulldogs for their cute wrinkles. However, those wrinkles need special care to prevent **infection**. Most owners use baby wipes to clean between the wrinkles.

A bulldog's coat is easy to care for. Its short hair does not need a lot of brushing.

Bathe bulldogs once a month at most. Too many baths can make their skin dry and itchy.

Bulldogs need a good veterinarian. The vet can provide health exams and **vaccines**. He or she can also **spay** or **neuter** a dog.

Puppies will need to see the vet several times during their first few months. Adult dogs should visit the vet once a year for a checkup.

Did you know?

Bulldogs tend to have bad breath. Owners should clean their teeth regularly.

Take care when traveling with a bulldog. Bulldogs have trouble breathing on airplanes.

Every dog needs a collar with identification tags. A **microchip** can also keep a bulldog safe. This way, an owner can find the pet if it gets lost.

At home, a crate offers a bulldog a place to rest. It can also help with housebreaking puppies.

Always watch a bulldog while he or she is near the water. Bulldogs are not good swimmers. Its big head and short legs make it hard to stay afloat.

PUPPIES

A bulldog mother is **pregnant** for about 63 days. Then, she gives birth to a **litter** of about four puppies.

All puppies are born blind and deaf. After two weeks, they can see and hear. At three weeks, the puppies begin taking their first steps.

Most bulldog puppies come from a breeder. Because they are so popular, few bulldogs are found at animal shelters.

THINGS THEY NEED

At eight to 12 weeks old, bulldog puppies are ready for **adoption**. When a puppy comes home, the owner should begin obedience training as soon as it is settled.

Bulldog puppies like to be active. So, they need daily exercise and training. A bulldog will be a loving companion for ten to 12 years.

Otto the bulldog earned a Guinness World Record! He rode his skateboard through a tunnel made up of 30 people.

GLOSSARY

adoption the process of taking responsibility for a pet.

American Kennel Club (AKC) an organization that studies and promotes interest in purebred dogs.

ancestor a family member from an earlier time.

breed a group of animals sharing the same appearance and features. To breed is to produce animals by mating.

brindle having dark streaks or spots on a gray or brownish background.

Canidae (KAN-uh-dee) the scientific Latin name for the dog family. Members of this family are called canids. They include wolves, jackals, foxes, coyotes, and domestic dogs.

fawn a light grayish brown.

infection (ihn-FEHK-shuhn) the causing of an unhealthy condition by something harmful, such as bacteria.

litter all of the puppies born at one time to a mother dog.

mascot something to bring good luck and help cheer on a team.

microchip an electronic circuit placed under an animal's skin. A microchip contains identifying information that can be read by a scanner.

neuter (NOO-tuhr) to remove a male animal's reproductive glands.

nutrient (NOO-tree-uhnt) something found in food that living beings take in to live and grow.

piebald a pattern of pigmented spots on a white coat.

pregnant having one or more babies growing within the body.

spay to remove a female animal's reproductive organs.

vaccine (vak-SEEN) a shot given to prevent illness or disease.

ONLINE RESOURCES

Booklinks NONFICTION NETWORK
FREE! ONLINE NONFICTION RESOURCES

To learn more about bulldogs, visit **abdobooklinks.com**. These links are routinely monitored and updated to provide the most current information available.

INDEX